Proposition 1 – Houston Drainage Fee

IMPOSITION 1

PIE IN THE SKY

THE HOUSTON DRAINAGE FEE

A Treatise By Daniel W. Harbaugh,
Senior Citizen

Houston Drainage Fee – Pie-In-The-Sky

Buy *HOUSTON DRAINAGE FEE - PIE IN THE SKY* by Daniel W. Harbaugh (Paperback) online at Lulu.

www.lulu.com/.../houston-drainage-fee-pie-in-the-sky/.....

ISBN 978-1-300-65185-7

9 781300 651857

Houston Drainage Fee – Pie-In-The-Sky

FOREWORD: This is a 'Pie-In-The-Sky' tale of Proposition 1-Houston Drainage Fee. Improving Houston's flooding drainage system has merit and the touted '$5.00/month' fee is a reasonable price to pay; but the Proposition 1 scheme proves to be one big scam to pick the public's pockets. This monthly Drainage Fee was conceived, sponsored and financed by private-interest opportunists who stand to make $Mega-Millions from it; promoted by self-serving conflict-of-interest city politicians; and untruthfully foisted on the trusting voting public by a prevaricating Mayor who will reap vast campaign contributions from the perpetrators . The characters violate Federal, State and City laws with apparent immunity, and are sheltered from their law violations by 'Good Ol' Boys' in law enforcement. This book has names and irrefutable documentation to support the obvious conclusion:

HOUSTON, YOU'VE BEEN HAD!

COMMENTARY:

Obviously, laws are published in writing to provide the public, law breakers and law enforcers a positive source of information relevant to their activities. Per Texas Law:

"Campaign Finance Requirements for Texas Ballot Measures

The Texas Ethics Commission may engage civil action in a circuit court. If there is evidence of criminal wrongdoing, the complaint can be referred to the Attorney General for prosecution.

Specific-purpose committee

Under Texas law, any ballot measure group that is aimed at the passage or defeat of a ballot question is considered to be a specific-purpose committee. It is defined under the law as supporting or opposing one or more ballot measures defined by law.

The $100 cash rule

No individual contributor can donate more than $100 in cash to a specific purpose committee during a actual reporting period."

Houston Drainage Fee – Pie-In-The-Sky

Of the 48 originators of and contributors to 'Proposition 1/Renew Houston', an obvious Specific Purpose Committee, only one complied with the $100 rule; the rest funded it with a total $636,359. This sum is $631,559 more than the law allows.

I called this to the attention of the Houston City Attorney, the Harris County District Attorney, the Texas Ethics Committee and the Texas Attorney General, Greg Abbott. Only Mr. Abbott had the common courtesy to reply; stating it was a matter for the Texas Ethics Committee.

My point is 'The Law is the Law' and failure of law enforcers to enforce the law is a dereliction of duty detrimental to the public interest.

My goal is to see passage of Proposition 1/Drainage Fee be declared invalid due to unlawful promotion by 'Renew Houston'. I have no objecting to it being placed on the next ballot where the voters now know what they are voting for.

Houston Drainage Fee – Pie-In-The-Sky

PIE-IN-THE-SKY ...
THE HOUSTON DRAINAGE FEE

Proposition 1 is a **'PIE-IN-THE-SKY'** scheme to enrich the private-sector sponsors. The **'SKY'** is the dubious 'one-size-fits-all' satellite imaging technique for determining impervious surfaces and the **'PIE'** is the financial feast by the sponsors on the public's money. The originator of this Drainage Fee scheme, **'Renew Houston, Inc.'**, is a private corporation, not a public agency of the City of Houston. Members of this organization will benefit financially by contracting with the City for the drainage work. They publicly tout they anticipate over $125 Million in revenues from Proposition 1 drainage work in FY 2012

The City of Houston, via provably error-prone interpretation of physical facts and much imagination, classifies virtually all areas on a residential property other than satellite interpretation green lawn as **'impervious surface'**; and charges a monthly Drainage Fee based on the total sq. ft. area of their definition of 'impervious surface'.

7

THE CART BEFORE THE HORSE ...

Nowhere in the whole Proposition 1 sales-pitch was there any mention of any plan on what, where and how Houston's drainage problem is to be solved. The satellite imaging gimmick merely points out revenue sources - get all the money and then figure out how to spend it.

About any 4th year civil engineering class could compile a master plan for Houston's drainage problems; utilizing USGS photo-maps showing topography and all structures, plus ask any realtor or insurance agent where Houston floods. The Houston Public Works & Engineering Dept. could then determine and prioritize remedial drainage projects on the basis of physical need, not political favoritism.

Proposition 1 Drainage Fee was not based on prior observations by the City of Houston Public Works & Engineering Department that the City's drainage system requires, quote, **"complete rebuilding"** in excess of normal maintenance and routine improvements; in fact, the City PWE has done an excellent job to date on the City's drainage needs.

8

Houston Drainage Fee – Pie-In-The-Sky

Proposition 1 Drainage Fee was peddled to the public as a flood control endeavor. No major flooding in Houston history has occurred except during heavy rapid rainfall. Houston's floods are **'flash floods'** of a few hours duration; residents don't wade around in water for days or weeks as in Midwest etc. floods.

Houston elevations above sea level range from 97-ft at International Airport Houston, 50-ft downtown Houston, 46-ft Hobby Airport, 32-ft Ellington Airport, and 20-ft NASA/ Clear Lake. This 77-ft drop over the 33-miles is an average 'slope' of 0.005303-inches per foot, and an unchallengeable basis for flooding conditions in a heavy rainfall, and Proposition 1 can do little about it.

Mother Nature provided Houston with a natural drainage system via bayous. Outside of keeping these bayous clear, little else will assist Houston's drainage except creating flood water retention ponds and ditches to them. Locating sites and excavating holes in the ground is well within duties and capabilities of the PWE, and does not require expensive private cohorts.

Houston Drainage Fee – Pie-In-The-Sky

Proposition 1 Drainage Fee was sold the voters on the 2010 ballot based on a fee for the total square feet of **"actual impervious surface"**.

"CITY OF HOUSTON STATEMENT OF PRINCIPLES PROPOSED MUNICIPAL STREET AND DRAINAGE UTILITY SYSTEM

V. Calculation of Drainage Fee. A. Impervious Surface ("Hard Area") All fees will be based on square footage of **actual impervious surface** (hard area) on the property, which will be determined by the use of digitized mapping data. "Impervious surface" means any area that does not readily absorb water, such as buildings, decks, patios, driveways, and other paved areas."

Point Of Fact:

There is no provision in the English language, and certainly none in 'legal-speak' English, for interpreting the word **'actual'** as having any other meaning; an **'actual impervious surface'** is exactly that. The criteria for determining actual impervious surfaces should be left to Engineers, not politicians.

Houston Drainage Fee – Pie-In-The-Sky

About everything but grass lawn is designated by the City as impervious. It is a provable fact that any ordinary Houston grass lawn will reach a surface saturation point in a time interval of rainfall; typically ranging from a few minutes to a few hours, depending on the intensity and quantity of rainfall. After the surface saturation point is reached there is no further water retention, and the lawn area is just as 'impervious' as any actual impervious surface, such as concrete pavement. If the City uses grass lawn as the criteria for 'pervious surface', then any similarly pervious surface, such as crushed concrete, shell or gravel driveways or parking areas, cannot logically be classified as an 'impervious surface'. Any surface that will readily grow grass is obviously not impervious.

Point Of Interest:
One would assume that the Mayor of Houston has sufficient brains to ascertain the accuracy of her information prior to mouthing same.
The Mayor, representing the City, has not complied with her own broadcast and published advertising wordage used to sell Proposition 1 to the voters. **This constitutes a violation of Texas Law:**

Houston Drainage Fee – Pie-In-The-Sky

Mayor Annise Parker publicly advertised and sold this scheme to the voters as an **'average $5.00 per month fee'** for a residential property. Most average residential property owners are now finding their drainage fee is vastly higher than the average. Small business owners, the real backbone of Houston's economy, are stuck with absurd extravagantly high drainage fees. The Houston Chronicle reports that Parker now says the average estimate of $5 a month she used to sell voters on the fee was wrong. The mayor revised that estimate to an average of $8.25 per month, a 65 percent increase; and Parker publicly apologized for mistakenly understating the typical monthly fee during the campaign.

Texas Occupations Code - Section 101.201.

§ 101.201. FALSE, MISLEADING, OR DECEPTIVE ADVERTISING.

(a) A person may not use advertising that is false, misleading, deceptive, or not readily subject to verification.

Houston Drainage Fee – Pie-In-The-Sky

Proposition 1 Drainage Fee cannot replace the **Laws of Physics,** including gravity and fluid-flow. The City's only legitimate concern is with that water flowing off a property into the City drainage system. The area of any structure not in direct contact with the surface of the ground, and with no barriers to surface water flowing under it, is not an 'impervious surface'. Only the actual on-ground coverage footprints, such as rooftops, slabs, piers, and pavements are a valid impervious surface. Rainwater will flow first to the nearest on-grade ground surface area, such as under on-pier structures, before it will flow off the property. Parked cars, RV camper trailers, semi- trailers, boat trailers, fire wood piles, shade trees, bare dirt, clothes on the clothesline, lawn chairs, etc., are all now classified as impervious.

Houston Drainage Fee – Pie-In-The-Sky

IMPERVIOUS SURFACES: A random sampling of the subject on 'Google':

New York City Watershed Regulations Impervious Surfaces: Pavement, concrete, asphalt, roofs or other hard surfacing material. **Impervious** surfaces do **not** include: dirt, shell, crushed stone, wood decking or gravel …

Florida : "A few decades ago, crushed shell and hard sand driveways were the norm in Florida. They were permeable and allowed water to sink into the ground naturally. Over the years we've moved away from shell driveways for aesthetic reasons …"

Pennsylvania: Green Options for Driveways – A permeable driveway can be created in many ways: pavers, permeable concrete, crushed stone and crushed seashells are the most popular.

Comment: New York, Florida and Pennsylvania are all considered technologically sufficiently advanced to conclude crushed stone, crushed concrete, crushed shell and gravel are **permeable surfaces**. The City of Houston, obviously, needs to go back to school.

14

Houston Drainage Fee – Pie-In-The-Sky

CRUSHED CONCRETE DRIVEWAY TESTS

Utilizing my qualifications and experience as a California State University/Long Beach graduate Geotechnical Engineer, I conducted 'Porosity' and 'Percolation' tests on my crushed concrete driveway. These tests show the permeability of water on the driveway. This driveway was installed by my 80+ year old self using a wheelbarrow, shovel and a rake to spread a pile of crushed concrete material to an average 3-inches thickness over a previous grass lawn area. The City labels this driveway an 'impervious surface' for their drainage fee.

The lawn areas are a few inches of topsoil over typical Houston area clay. The same 'Porosity' and 'Percolation' tests, as conducted on the crushed concrete driveway, run on an undisturbed lawn area, shows the lawn is far more 'impervious' than the crushed concrete driveway. The City designates the lawn as the standard for 'pervious'; therefore, the only logical criteria this crushed concrete driveway has to meet is be as 'pervious', or 'impervious', as the lawn.

INCONGRUITY ...

Houston has over 360 'high-rise 'buildings, the majority in downtown Houston. The JP Morgan Chase Tower is 1,002-ft tall. The Wells Fargo Plaza is 992-ft tall. There are 43 other skyscrapers higher than 400-ft.

These building are charged a Proposition 1 drainage fee based on their roof area and on-ground 'impervious surfaces'. Any Houstonians smart enough to shut their windows in a big rain storm obviously realizes rain doesn't usually fall straight down. The JP Morgan Chase Tower side to the weather, about 3-1/2 football fields in size, is obviously an 'impervious surface' and the rain water hitting same is going to flow into the City drainage system; all in addition to the rain falling directly on the roof and grounds of the site. The building itself does not shield an equivalent rainless shadow area on ground on the lee side of weather.

Too bad, for the Proposition 1 pushers, that they missed this drainage fee gold mine.

My initial attempts **to 'Request an Appeal of your Drainage Verification'** via www.rebuildhouston.com were fruitless. **"The system could not locate address ..."** . Never mind that **'Braniff ST'** is exactly that

posted on the City's street signs. The City is apparently so incompetent that they can't locate **Braniff ST**, with both Hobby Airport and the Houston Fire Academy on it.

I afterwards submitted my request for drainage fee correction, including all engineering data sufficient to justify it, to Mayor Parker and Daniel W. Krueger, P.E., PWE. Neither had the common courtesy to reply.

Houston Drainage Fee – Pie-In-The-Sky

At this writing, January 2013, I have submitted, to both Mr. Krueger and the Mayor, an appeal to my provable-excessive monthly drainage charge, complete with satellite images and explanation of all structures as to 'impervious' designations. The appeal included the following premises:

PREMISES:

(A) Only such surfaces in actual 'foot-print' contact with the ground are valid as 'Impervious'.

(B) Only the ground water flow off the property into the city drainage system is a valid consideration.

(C) Only such surfaces that are actually 'Impervious' by standard engineering definitions are valid.

Since all of the above Premises curtail the City's current drainage fee banditry, I anticipate this appeal will be ignored too.

Houston Drainage Fee – Pie-In-The-Sky

In my particular case, my residential property is provably an almost 'Net-Zero 'contributor to Houston's drainage system, and entitled, at least, to the promised average $5/monthly drainage fee.

My house was built in 1946 on small concrete piers with floor-level 2-ft above the bare ground. In the 66+ ensuing years, the process of lawn-mowing and decay of the clippings there from has raised the lawn topsoil level to over 4-inchs above the bare under-house ground, creating a natural 'retention-pond'. The City is apparently unaware of the topsoil creation process; undoubtedly attributing it to God having his minions truck it in and elves spreading it out over Houston's clay. Per the Law-Of-Physics/Gravity and physical proximity, water will flow to under my house before it will flow into Houston's roadside ditch.

My later-added crushed concrete circular drive, applied over the already raised sod area, fronting the house from lot-line to lot-line, is both a permeable surface by standard engineering criteria and a dike directing rainwater under the house and thus hindering it flowing into the City ditch.

Additionally, I have a 4-ft deep x 8-ft x 32-ft above-ground swimming pool that collects its water from the roof of my house via gutters and downspouts; a 'retention-pond' by any criteria. Except in summer swim-season when we occasionally top it off with the garden hose, the pool water-level ranges from about 2-ft to 3-ft; the low levels due to evaporation; another process the City is apparently unaware of.

The few actually 'impervious' surfaces on my property, including my 2-car garage, a house front-entry walkway, a backyard workshop, and a patio deck, all total within the $5/month average drainage fee.

INTEGRITY , ETHICS ? Anyone?

'Renew Houston', a **'Specific Purpose Committee'** under Texas Statutes, was created solely to influence the passage of Houston ballot measure 'Proposition 1' Drainage Fee. In the list of contributors in prima facie in violation of Texas Statutes and Houston Codes covering financing ballot measures, none stands out more blatantly than **Houston City Councilman Stephen Costello**; a 'public official' funding over $80,000 and pushing a ballot measure he authored that will greatly enrich him personally.

CITY OF HOUSTON – CODE OF ORDINANCES – CHAPTER 18

WHEREAS, Chapter 18 of the Code of Ordinances currently contains several provisions that serve as general guidelines in addressing impermissible conduct of city officials; and

WHEREAS, it is the policy of the city that all city officials shall conduct themselves with integrity and credibility in a manner consistent with the best interests of the city and the public's trust; and

WHEREAS, the city is steadfast in its endeavors to strengthen the ethics standards applicable to city officials in an effort to eliminate conflicts of interest and opportunities for city officials to derive any personal gain or advantage as a result of their status as a city official, including the provision of any preferential treatment to any person, business, or organization in whose welfare the city official is directly interested; and

WHEREAS, it is recommended that City Council adopt the proposed amendments to Chapter 18 to provide greater transparency, increased awareness, and a heightened standard of accountability concerning the ethics standards incumbent upon all city officials in their service to the city and its citizens;

NOW THEREFORE,
BE IT ORDAINED BY THE CITY COUNCIL OF THE CITY OF HOUSTON, TEXAS:

Section 1. That the findings contained in the preamble of this Ordinance are determined to be true and correct and are hereby adopted as a part of this Ordinance.
Section 2. That Sections 18-1,18-2 and 18-3 of the Code of Ordinances, Houston, Texas, are hereby amended to read as follows:

Sec. 18-3. Standards of conduct.

(a) It shall be unlawful for any city official to:
(1) Engage in any business or professional activity that conflicts with the discharge of official duties.

(2) Invest or hold any investment or interest in any financial, business, commercial or other transaction that creates a conflict between the public trust held as an official of the city and the official's private interests.

Per Houston City Attorney, David Feldman:

"Mission Statement: Integrity & Candor - Acting with a commitment to honesty and ethical behavior,"

I submitted the particulars on Councilman Costello's quite obvious conflict-of-interest and statute violations to Mr. Feldman, and he wasn't interested; suggesting I direct my efforts elsewhere. I then pointed out that ordinary Houston citizens don't have to call the Police Chief to report their car stolen; any officer of the law will suffice; and, per his 'commitment', he should be capable of forwarding my complaint to the proper authorities.

I then submitted my complaint to the Harris County District Attorney; he wasn't interested. Since violations of Texas Statues on ballot measures are involved, I copied all my submissions to Texas Attorney General Greg Abbott; he wasn't interested either.

It's a sad day for the citizens of Houston when enforcement of the law is controlled by public servant 'good old boys' covering up for each other.

RENEW HOUSTON, INC.
Renew Houston, Inc. was formed as an IRS nonprofit corporation in March 2009 and is headquartered in the offices of the Houston Council of Engineering Companies at 2180 North Loop West, Suite 221, Houston, TX 77018. Their stated purpose on IRS Form 990 is: **"Education of the general public …"** and **"Survey of the general public …"** No mention of the fact that the members stand to collectively make mega-millions of dollars on Proposition 1 Drainage Fee; undoubtedly a mere accidental oversight.

Houston Drainage Fee – Pie-In-The-Sky

Form **990-EZ**

Department of the Treasury
Internal Revenue Service

Short Form
Return of Organization Exempt From Income Tax

Under section 501(c), 527, or 4947(a)(1) of the Internal Revenue Code (except black lung benefit trust or private foundation)

▶ Sponsoring organizations of donor advised funds and controlling organizations as defined in section 512(b)(13) must file Form 990. All other organizations with gross receipts less than $500,000 and total assets less than $1,250,000 at the end of the year may use this form

▶ The organization may have to use a copy of this return to satisfy state reporting requirements.

OMB No 1545-1150

2009

Open to Public Inspection

A For the 2009 calendar year, or tax year beginning _____ and ending _____

B Check if applicable:
- Address change
- Name change
- [X] Initial return
- Terminated
- Amended return
- Application pending

Please use IRS label or print or type. See Specific Instructions.

C Name of organization
Renew Houston, Inc.

Number and street (or P O box, if mail is not delivered to street address) Room/suite
2180 N. Loop West, Suite 221

City or town, state or country, and ZIP + 4
Houston, TX 77018

D Employer identification number
26-4673522

E Telephone number
713-426-0800

F Group Exemption Number ▶

● Section 501(c)(3) organizations and 4947(a)(1) nonexempt charitable trusts must attach a completed Schedule A (Form 990 or 990-EZ)

G Accounting method [X] Cash ☐ Accrual
Other (specify) ▶

I Website: ▶ N/A

H Check ▶ ☐ if the organization is not required to attach Schedule B (Form 990, 990-EZ, or 990-PF)

J Tax-exempt status (check only one) — [X] 501(c) (4) ◀ (insert no) ☐ 4947(a)(1) or ☐ 527

K Check ▶ ☐ if the organization is not a section 509(a)(3) supporting organization and its gross receipts are normally not more than $25,000 A Form 990-EZ or Form 990 return is not required, but if the organization chooses to file a return, be sure to file a complete return

L Add lines 5b, 6b, and 7b, to line 9 to determine gross receipts, if $500,000 or more, file Form 990 instead of Form 990-EZ ▶ $ | 115,279

Part I Revenue, Expenses, and Changes in Net Assets or Fund Balances (See the instructions for Part I)

1	Contributions, gifts, grants, and similar amounts received	1	115,279

Form 990-EZ (2009)   Renew Houston, Inc.   26-4673522   Page 2

Part III Statement of Program Service Accomplishments (See the instructions for Part III)

What is the organization's primary exempt purpose? See Statement 2

Describe what was achieved in carrying out the organization's exempt purposes. In a clear and concise manner, describe the services provided, the number of persons benefited, and other relevant information for each program title.

Expenses
(Required for section 501(c)(3) and 501(c)(4) organizations and section 4947(a)(1) trusts, optional for others)

28 Education of general public with presentations on Renew Houston's purpose and goals.

(Grants $ _____) If this amount includes foreign grants, check here ▶ ☐ | 28a | 42,000.

29 Survey of the general public regarding the major initiatives of Renew Houston

(Grants $ _____) If this amount includes foreign grants, check here ▶ ☐ | 29a | 19,500.

30 _____

(Grants $ _____) If this amount includes foreign grants, check here ▶ ☐ | 30a |

31 Other program services (attach schedule)

(Grants $ _____) If this amount includes foreign grants, check here ▶ ☐ | 31a |

32 Total program service expenses (add lines 28a through 31a) ▶ | 32 | 61,500.

Part IV List of Officers, Directors, Trustees, and Key Employees. List each one even if not compensated (See the instructions for Part IV)

Per Texas Ethics Code:

INCORPORATED POLITICAL COMMITTEES

In general, corporations are prohibited from making political contributions or other political expenditures. A political committee may incorporate for liability purposes only, however, without subjecting itself to the prohibitions on corporate political expenditures. To incorporate for liability purposes only, a political committee may provide in its official incorporation documents that it is a political committee that is incorporating for liability purposes only and that its only principal purpose is to accept political contributions and make political expenditures.

The 'Renew Houston, Inc.' IRS document submitted to create a 'non-profit corporation' makes no mention of 'for liability purposes only'. **The only 'liability' evident is the corporate membership is liable to get vastly richer from it.**

Houston Drainage Fee – Pie-In-The-Sky

The principal authors and pushers of Proposition 1 are J.R. 'Bob' Jones and City Councilman Stephen Costello; it is, of course, just an impartial coincidence that their engineering firms will make $Mega-Millions from it.

Houston Drainage Fee – Pie-In-The-Sky

"Specific-purpose committee: Under Texas law, any ballot measure group that is aimed at the passage or defeat of a ballot question is considered to be a **specific-purpose committee**. It is defined under the law as supporting or opposing one or more ballot measures defined by law.

The $100 cash rule No individual contributor can donate more than $100 in cash to a specific purpose committee during an actual reporting period."

The originator of this Drainage Fee scheme, **'Renew Houston, Inc.'**, is a **'Specific–Purpose Committee'**. They funded $636,359.00 to put Proposition 1 on the ballot in 2010.

All but one, Neil Brooks, of the 'Renew Houston, Inc.' contributors, listed in the following pages, violated Texas Law on contributions to a 'Specific Purpose Committee'.

Houston Drainage Fee – Pie-In-The-Sky

Date	Name	Amount
06/11/2010	Binkley & Barfield	$ 2,500.00
06/15/2010	Asian American Engineers Architects	$ 250.00
06/15/2010	Nathelyne Kennedy & Associates	$ 1,500.00
06/17/2010	ESPA Corporation, Inc.	$ 5,000.00
06/21/2010	Raba-Kistner Consulting	$ 2,000.00
06/21/2010	Boyer & Associates	$ 10,000.00
06/25/2010	Stanley Spurling & Hamilton, Inc.	$ 2,500.00
07/02/2010	BRH-Garver Construction, L.P.	$ 10,000.00
07/02/2010	Cherry Crushed Concrete Co.	$ 5,000.00
07/02/2010	Malcolm Pirnie	$ 1,000.00
07/06/2010	El Dorado Paving Company, Inc.	$ 500.00
07/06/2010	Mickie Service Company, Inc.	$ 1,000.00
07/07/2010	Schaumburg & Polk, Inc.	$ 500.00
07/08/2010	Calco Contracting, Ltd	$ 1,000.00
07/08/2010	American Society of Indian Engineers	$ 500.00
07/08/2010	Texas Sterling Construction, LP	$ 10,000.00
07/14/2010	ROMCO Equipment Co	$ 2,500.00

Houston Drainage Fee – Pie-In-The-Sky

Date	Name	Amount
05/11/2010	Van De Wiele & Vogler	$ 5,000.00
05/14/2010	HDR Engineering, Inc.	$ 5,000.00
05/18/2010	Neal Brooks	$ 5.00
05/24/2010	Brown & Gay Engineers, Inc.	$ 5,000.00
05/25/2010	Bury+Partners	$ 1,500.00
05/27/2010	Isani Consultants, Inc.	$ 1,000.00
06/03/2010	United Engineers	$ 3,000.00
06/03/2010	RS&H	$ 3,000.00
06/03/2010	C. Richard Everett	$ 5,000.00
06/03/2010	ARCADIS US, Inc.	$ 2,500.00
06/03/2010	Tolunay-Wong Engineers	$ 250.00
06/04/2010	William Calhoun	$ 300.00
06/04/2010	Linda Stuckey	$ 5,000.00
06/07/2010	Slack & Co.	$ 5,000.00
06/07/2010	HNTB Corporation	$ 1,000.00
06/08/2010	Cobb, Fendley & Associates	$ 6,000.00
06/09/2010	LAN Engineering	$ 5,000.00

Houston Drainage Fee – Pie-In-The-Sky

Date	Name	Amount
07/14/2010	Wilbur Smith Associates	$ 750.00
07/21/2010	Associated Steel Fabricators, Inc.	$ 1,000.00
07/21/2010	Shrader Engineering Inc.	$ 1,500.00
07/21/2010	Steven Jarvis	$ 1,000.00
07/27/2010	Huff & Mitchell, Inc.	$ 5,000.00
07/27/2010	Excalibur Excavation, LP	$ 1,000.00
07/27/2010	Lodge Lumber Co., Inc.	$ 500.00
08/04/2010	R.G. Miller Engineers	$ 2,500.00
08/17/2010	Montgomery & Barnes	$ 1,500.00
		$ 336,359.00
LOANS:		
05/17/2010	Stephen Costello	$ 50,000.00
05/19/2010	Jones & Carter, Inc.	$ 140,000.00
06/08/2010	Jeff E. Ross	$ 25,000.00
06/08/2010	J R Jones	$ 30,000.00
06/11/2010	Stephen Costello	$ 30,000.00
06/17/2010	Edwin Friedrichs	$ 25,000.00
		$ 300,000.00

Houston Drainage Fee – Pie-In-The-Sky

 All the contributors were, of course, just civic-minded personages interested only in improving the quality of life in Houston.

Houston City Councilman Stephen Costello
Funded 'Renew Houston,Inc.' $90,000
Costello Inc. participated in $55 Million in city contracts
You'd Smile Too !
Smells like roses?

PIE-IN-THE-SKY
HOUSTON DRAINAGE FEE

'RENEW HOUSTON' / RENEW YOUR BANKROLL
THE PUBLIC PAYS ...WE PROFIT !
GET ON THE GRAVY TRAIN
BUY A POLITICIAN TODAY

THE VICTORS GLOAT …

Houston Drainage Fee – Pie-In-The-Sky

BRH-GARVER CONSTRUCTION, L.P.
BRH Contracting, LLC, General Partner
7600 S. Santa Fe. Bldg. A-1 East
Houston, Texas 77061
Phone: 713-921-2929 Fax: 713-921-2487

December 13, 2010

Dear HCA Members:

ReNew Houston has a fundraiser scheduled to pay off the remaining debt for the November 2010 Charter Amendment effort. Mayor Parker will be in attendance. See the attached flyer.

This effort was funded 90% by our engineering community and only 10% by the contracting community. This proposition MIRACULOUSLY passed. It will generate annually $125mm of engineering and construction in years to some for correcting vital flooding drainage and street issues.

The engineering work will amount to roughly 10% of the expenditure and construction contracts will be 90%. When our market corrects we should see construction profits of five ($5) to ten ($10) mm per year from this effort. When our market corrects we should realize profits equal to the entire engineering revenue. Without this amendment our market would be much slower to correct.

When streets and drainage are redone all utilities are impacted, all members of HCA are positively impacted. This includes suppliers and contractors. BRH-Garver is experiencing our 2nd losing year in our 38 year history yet we have contributed a total of $20,000.00 to this effort as has Slack and Company. The total pledge from HCA to retire this dept is only $25,000.00 so far. We need your help to keep our organization from being embarrassed at the fund raiser tomorrow night and because it is the right thing to do.

Please email your pledge to Jeff Nielson and try to attend the event at Jeff Ross' home. We should carry the bulk of the $200,000.00 goal to retire the ReNew Houston debt.

Hope to see you Tuesday evening.

Mike Sun

34

Join Mayor Annise Parker
to Celebrate the Passage of Proposition 1
to ReNew Houston and Pay off the Campaign debt!

Place: Home of Doris Williams and Jeff Ross
        1821 Sunset Boulevard, Houston, TX 77005
Date: Tuesday, December 14, 2010
        5:30 p.m. until 7:00 p.m.

RESPONSE FORM

_____ Yes, I will attend the reception and join Mayor Parker to celebrate a great victory and help pay off the campaign debt to 'ReNew Houston'.

Enclosed is my check for:

_____ $25,000 Co-Chairman _____ $10,000 Underwriter _____ $5,000 Sponsor _____ $2,500 Patron

_____ $1,000 Host _____ Other *Corporate, personal and PAC contributions may be accepted.*

MEDIA RESPONSE

The Media responded to the facts of Proposition 1 Drainage Fee, noting Reliant Stadium will pay an annual Drainage Fee of $418,000, Bush and Hobby Airports will pay $6 Million, Port of Houston will pay $200,000; and the total annual fee of all such city property will be $9.2 Million.

All these fees are paid by the public in increased costs for using these facilities, in addition to paying their own drainage fees.
Can you spell 'RIP-OFF'?

Houston drainage fee bills catch some by surprise

More uproar as drainage bills arrive
Some critics call mayor's repeated use of $5 average fee misleading

Houston Chronicle May 21, 2011

Manuel Menocal thought the sample drainage bill he received Thursday would tell him he owed the city $5. After all, it was the number repeatedly used by Mayor Annise Parker and proponents of Proposition 1 during the fall campaign for a drainage fee.

When the Clear Lake man opened the bill, it was more than double that — $12.16 a month.

"It's the same thing as having them knock on your door, and when you answer there's someone with a pistol saying 'Pay up!' " Menocal said.

The May surprise delivered in city envelopes is the latest controversy in a public policy matter that has caused an uproar at every turn.

Seven months ago, voters narrowly passed an amendment to the city charter imposing a drainage fee on Houstonians for the next 20 years to rebuild the curbs, gutters and streets of a flood-prone city. Llast month, a divided council passed an ordinance to implement the fee over the objections of county government officials and nonprofit agencies who wanted exemptions, as well as those of church and school leaders who sought a more absolute exemption than the one granted them.

Harris County Treasurer Orlando Sanchez said Friday that the fee could not have come at a worse time for the county.

"It is the most inopportune time for the city to delve into the county coffers," he said. "I'm not crazy about having one taxing agency tax another to help it out of its fiscal crises."

Proper stewardship of dollars meant for infrastructure repairs would have made the ballot proposition unnecessary, said Sanchez, a former city councilman.

$418,000 tab

The city's ordinance states that the county would have to pay for properties that generate revenue, such as the Reliant Stadium complex. Based on the city's fee rate of 3.2 cents per square foot of impervious cover, the county would be on the hook for $418,000 annually, thanks to the roughly 300 acres of impervious cover at the Reliant complex, home to the Astrodome, Reliant Stadium, other structures and vast parking lots.

Parker stuck to the $5 number for homeowners as honest and accurate this week during a news conference.

"I'm hearing from folks, and I'm sure the council members are, as well, that 'Oh, we thought the drainage fee was going to be $5.' We have been very, very clear in all of our communications, and that is that we try to get a representative house situation to express to the citizens what it would be," Parker said. "Somehow, to a lot of folks, that translated into everybody is going to pay $5. No, you pay based on the amount of impervious cover you have, which is the fairest way to do it."

Houston Drainage Fee – Pie-In-The-Sky

Andy Icken, the city's chief development officer and one of the officials who helped establish the rate structure, said the city used two different methodologies that each produced an average of 1,875 square feet of impervious cover that accounted, not just for homes, but for driveways and other structures.

There was no strategy to try to sell the public on a low-ball figure, Icken said, but "the city would like to keep the fee as low as we can, constrained by the need to raise $125 million" from property owners as mandated by Proposition 1.

Protest planned

Menocal's home is only 1,636 square feet, but he has a garage and a driveway that have the city billing him for a total of 4,561 square feet. He disagreed with the city's calculations and said he plans to file a protest. He said city officials' use of the $5-a-month average was misleading.

Councilman Mike Sullivan said the city should have used a range to describe the possible hit to homeowners' pocketbooks.

The city presented a range of possible monthly bills at 10 capital improvement project meetings in February. Parker continued to use the $5 figure this week.

"The charges are anywhere from three to six times what the proponents of the referendum said they would be, and, frankly, the city, as well," Sullivan said. "My personal feeling is, it was not a realistic estimate of what an average citizen's lot would cost."

Icken said city officials consistently couched the $5 figure as an average, that not everybody would pay the same thing.

"What people heard, I can't say," Icken said.

Houston Drainage Fee – Pie-In-The-Sky

Parker admits estimate wrong on drainage fee. Now says bill for the average resident would be more than $8

CHRIS MORAN
, HOUSTON CHRONICLE | June 7, 2011

Mayor Annise Parker acknowledged Tuesday that her administration erred in telling voters that the average homeowner's monthly Proposition 1 drainage fee would be $5. It is actually closer to $8.25, she said.

Parker said that among the options she will send to the Houston City Council to make up for the error is to lower homeowners' bills to the $5 average.

The disclosure comes weeks before the city sends out the first bills to help pay for the $8 billion, 20-year plan to shore up its drainage infrastructure that voters narrowly approved last November. And it follows weeks of complaints from homeowners who got sample bills for a monthly charge two, three or more times as high as the one frequently used in the Proposition 1 campaign.

"The typical example we used may have given the wrong impression to the voters and to Council," Parker said. "I'm going to lay out to Council ways to bring (the rate) it down. I think we probably ought to do that, but Council will need to do this with me."

Houston Drainage Fee – Pie-In-The-Sky

'Now we've got proof'

Opponents of the drainage fee seized on the admission as evidence that voters were misled.

"Now we've got proof that we have been lied to," said former county Tax Assessor Paul Bettencourt, who is assisting plaintiffs who have filed suit against the city to overturn the fee because, they allege, the ballot language was misleading. A superior court judge dismissed the suit.

"She hasn't been coming clean with the public and telling them what they need to know," Bettencourt said of Parker. "We got an appeal and this is certainly going to add some significant juice to it."

The proposition calls for the city to raise $125 million a year through a monthly drainage fee. To raise the money, the city estimated the average lot size and impervious cover — an area that does not absorb water - and estimated how much it would have to charge homeowners and business owners to reach that threshold.

After the outcry triggered by sample bills sent to households last month, the Chronicle sent a public information request to the city asking for figures on how many households have received sample monthly bills that exceed $5 and how many received bills of less than $5.

Houston Drainage Fee – Pie-In-The-Sky

Though those figures have not yet been provided, the mayor said the city has already found that many more bills were going out for more than $5 than for less than $5.

Average lot is larger

The average fee was based on what was touted as a typical Houston residential property - a 5,000-square-foot lot with 1,875 square feet of impervious surface.

The city's revised estimate - again using satellite imagery and appraisal district data - is that the typical Houston home sits on a 7,500-square-foot lot with 2,850 square feet of impervious surface. That yields a monthly bill of approximately $8.25, Parker said.

Councilman C.O. "Brad" Bradford called the 65 percent increase over what people thought they were voting for "unacceptable" and "unconscionable." Bradford, who has continually questioned the fee and pushed for exemptions for churches and schools, said, "Now we're simply at a point, in my view, where it's time to start over."

But the city's charter can only be changed every two years, so instant repeal does not appear to be a legal option.

Parker said lowering bills to homeowners enough to stay true to the $5 average would leave the city $10 million to $12 million short of what it needs to collect as decreed by the proposition. She said the city could borrow that money to get through fiscal year 2012.

Houston Drainage Fee – Pie-In-The-Sky

Because the proposition requires only that the city reach $125 million through monthly drainage bills in the first year, the city could collect at the lower rate in 2013 and beyond without having to make up the difference through other sources.

Parker also said that Clear Lake residents will not have to pay the city of Houston's drainage fee at all.

Those residents already pay taxes to the Clear Lake City Water Authority for drainage service. Parker said that exempts them from the city-imposed fee, and explained that sample bills were sent to Clear Lake residents mistakenly last month.

chris.moran@chron.com

Parker lowering Houston drainage fee
Mayor says initial wrong estimate
makes adjustment a matter of 'trust'

Mayor Annise Parker is lowering the drainage fee that city property owners start paying next month after complaints from Houstonians receiving larger bills than the $5-a-month average advertised in last year's campaign to gain voter approval of the fee.

The mayor has ordered the Department of Public Works and Engineering to exempt 1,000 square feet of impervious surface at each property paying the fee. The mayor said reducing the amount of square footage in the assessment will lower the median bill from $8.25 a month to between $5 and $6.

Parker said she made the change "so that the drainage fees that voters expected to receive when they faced this item on the ballot last November are actually the fees that they will be paying moving into the future. It's about fairness. It's about trust."

Parker estimated last year that a typical home would pay about $5 a month. That estimate was appropriated by the Proposition 1 campaign, run in part by the political operatives who also run Parker's campaigns, and used in advertisements and promotions for the measure.

Last week, however, the mayor acknowledged that her staff was researching a public records request from the Houston Chronicle when they realized that the $5-a-month estimate was too low. The typical Houston home had close to 1,000 square feet more impervious surface than her administration previously had estimated.

The arrival of sample bills at homes last month touched off widespread anger among voters who claimed that they had been misled by last fall's campaign. Voters narrowly approved the misled by last fall's campaign. Voters narrowly approved the measure that creates a 20-year, $8 billion program to shore up the city's drainage system. On Thursday, Parker repeated her caveat that individual bills will vary. She also repeated her recommendation that people calculate their own bills and file a protest if they think they have been overcharged. She extended the deadline for filing a protest to the end of the year. "We want to make it right for the voters," Parker said. "This is about being fair to the voters who went out and voted for this program."

'Constant state of fixes'

Critics pounced on Thursday's announcement as the latest in a series of changes and mistakes in rolling out the controversial fee.

"She's just in a constant state of fixes," former county tax assessor Paul Bettencourt said of Parker. "This is not being done by public vote. This is not being done by council vote. It's being done by a mayor standing up at a press conference and saying, 'We're changing things.' "

City Councilman Mike Sullivan said the program continues to be beset by problems that include placing the onus on property owners to prove the city's mistakes on bills. He said lowering the bills has not assuaged his dissatisfaction.

"It is one concession on many still persistent problems that haven't been addressed," Sullivan declared.

Parker: City understands

He added a new problem to the list Thursday — the mayor's statement that the city may not raise the needed $125 million a year through the drainage fee, though that was the message of the pro-Proposition 1 campaign.

Houston Drainage Fee – Pie-In-The-Sky

Parker said lowering the bills will leave the city about $15 million short in fiscal year 2012. She proposes closing the gap by having the city's airport system and water utility system prepay next year's fees at a discount. After year one, she explained, the voter-approved charter amendment does not require that the city raise $125 million through the fee.

Bettencourt called that "borrowing," and said it was a violation of the program's pay-as-you-go mandate.

Parker said the prepayments would not constitute borrowing because the city would not pay the airport and water systems back.

As for the continuing criticism of the program, Parker said, voter approval of the fee in the midst of troubled economic times proves that Houstonians understand the importance of flood protection.

"We can't continue to grow as a city if we can't keep water out of people's homes and businesses. There is no free lunch," Parker said.

chris.moran@chron.com

Mayor Parker: "It's about fairness. It's about trust."   Yeah ... Sure ...

Nevermind the Bible ... use Proposition 1

Houston Drainage Fee – Pie-In-The-Sky

Ted Oberg

HOUSTON (KTRK) -- With some rain finally in the forecast, maybe it feels better to pay your brand new Houston drainage bill. The first rounds of those bills are due this month.

The program's unveiling was full of confusion and after digging through every single bill with the investigative group **Texas Watchdog**, we still have questions about who's paying what and why.

Let's get this out in the open right at the outset. Houston resident Clyde Bryan doesn't like the new drainage fee.

"They're employing voodoo science to get the job done," Bryan said.

When he showed us the drainage map for his street, houses are missing, driveways too; the street is jagged and he worries it's not accurately counting how much money each homeowner owes the city.

"It's like a bad science project at a high school," Bryan said.

For example, when Bryan called the city to verify his bill, he found out he didn't have one. The city counted his lot as part of his neighbor's.

"It's not voodoo science," said Tommy McClung with the City of Houston Public Works Department.

Houston Drainage Fee – Pie-In-The-Sky

The city blames any confusion on the speed in which it was all put together and promises to do better.

"Our view is get it right, be responsible, 'cause we want folks to know that, one, we may have gotten it wrong and two, if we have, we're going to get it right," McClung said.

But as the city races to raise money to improve drainage, is it too late? The city already wants your money and **our joint investigation with the team at Texas Watchdog** revealed a pretty murky system.

"Voters asked for this tax, drainage is a problem. We get that. How do you know if your institution, your school, your own home is being charged the right amount of money. I am not convinced we do know. I am not convinced the city knows," Texas Watchdog editor Trent Siebert said.

So far, more than 19,000 people, or about 4 percent of residents, have complained about their drainage bill. Houston Mayor Annise Parker says she's proud of the program, but admits there are problems.

"We are building the car while driving. This is light speed for a government entity to implement something this big and complicated this fast," Parker said.

When it comes to improving drainage, the numbers on the bill aren't all you're paying.

Houston Drainage Fee – Pie-In-The-Sky

The city is charging other government agencies - even other city departments - bills paid for by tax money or user fees, just moving from one government to another.

"A city taxing a city? That'd be like you taxing your wife," Bryan said.

And as a city department, Houston's airports can't put up a fight. The drainage fee for Bush, Hobby and Ellington airports is $6 million a year, every year.

The airports have a lot of concrete but no money trees. The cash comes from airport users, like you. You'll pay another $200,000 for the bill at the Port of Houston and at least another $500,000 more for the bill at Harris County-owned Reliant Center and even more to pay METRO's bill.

In Bryan's mind, it's good money down the drains, chasing the city's $125 million goal.

Long ago, the mayor and council decided the city should pay its fair share of the bill as well. But when we tallied up the city's share in the fund, we calculated $9.2 million, or about 7 percent of the entire fund, comes from taxpayers to pay the city's bill.

The biggest item is Bush Intercontinental Airport, which comes in at $3.8 million in drainage fees.

Cost of Houston Drainage Fee Angering City Homeowners

By Mark Whittington

Several months ago, the voters in the city of Houston narrowly voted in favor of a "drainage fee" that would be attached to city water bills that was advertised as being "an average" of five dollars per household.

However, according to the Houston Chronicle, a large number of Houston residents are opening their water bills and are finding that their drainage fees are somewhat higher than the advertised average, some more than double. Complaints are being made that the language in the voter proposition was misleading, leading people to believe that they would pay five dollars whereas many have wound up paying more.

The drainage fee is supposed to last twenty years and is designed to pay for repair of curbs, gutters and streets in Houston. Houston has a tendency to flood during strong rain storms, turning the streets into impassible rivers that swamp any passenger vehicle that tries to pass through them.

Part of the problem appears to be the way the drainage fee is calculated. Using satellite maps, the city of

Houston Drainage Fee – Pie-In-The-Sky

Houston has calculated the square feet of every homestead, including house, driveway, garage, and other structures such as pools, according to KHOU TV. Unfortunately some mistakes are being made, as city officials are now admitting, and some people are being overcharged.

In any case, when the proposition was put to the voters last fall, the figure of five dollars was used and most people assumed that would be the cost of the drainage fee. One suspects that had voters been aware that the figure was just an average and that many people would pay more, the proposition would not have passed.

Another controversy surrounding the drainage fee is the fact that it is not only hitting property owned by non profits, such as churches, but also property owned by Harris County, where Houston resides, such as Reliant Stadium, where the Houston Texans football team plays. Harris County is somewhat miffed that another governing body is taxing it.

Repealing the drainage fee may be an arduous process. A court case failed to overturn the fee on the basis of misleading language in the proposition. An effort to get the Texas legislature to overturn the drainage fee seems to have gotten nowhere. There will very likely be an effort to pressure the Houston City Council to either repeal or modify the drainage fee. In the meantime the infrastructure building effort that the drainage fee is to pay for invites the public to contest their drainage fee on its official website, Renew Houston."

Houston Drainage Fee – Pie-In-The-Sky

(KTRK) -- If you have a trampoline, trailer or boat in your yard, you could be paying more than your fair share of the city's new drainage fee.

The city of Houston is using satellite images of your yard to figure out the impervious surface, but that satellite image is mistaking all sorts of things as impervious surfaces.

We found all sorts of examples of mistakes made in calculating the drainage fee. If you do not appeal the errors, you are stuck paying for more impervious surfaces than you really have.

Barbara Stepanski's backyard is a playground for her grandchildren, complete with a trampoline.

"It is for the grandkids and they like it and they have always had the trampoline so they will have something to do," she said.

Unfortunately for Stepanski, when it comes to the new drainage fee, the city's satellite images see the trampoline, her trailer and tractor the same way it sees concrete -- as impervious surfaces

It's the very thing that is used to figure out how much money she owes unless she appeals the fee.

"I will go and see what I can do about that," said Stepanski. "That's not right."

Houston Drainage Fee – Pie-In-The-Sky

The satellite images are taken every other January, so if you have a car or boat in your backyard, check the rebuildhouston.org web site and see if it's accurate. While the appeals process has started, the Coalition for a Greater Houston is going to court to get the election overturned.

The coalition recently surveyed 600 voters about the fee. The group says about half of the respondents voted for the fee but now many have changed their minds.

"If they had known that certain groups were going to be exempted, they would have voted against the proposition 65 to 29," said former Harris County tax assessor Paul Bettencourt.

The city is asking a judge to throw out the lawsuit. Even so, officials admitted that errors on the maps are to be expected and that's why homeowners should take a close look at the satellite images of their property.

"There may, in fact, be some situations that citizens had something else that looked impervious to from the maps," said said Chief Development Officer Andy Icken. "We want them to correct it."

'Renew Houston, Inc.' morphed into **'Rebuild Houston'**. The 'Rebuild Houston Oversight Committee' has 9 members; 5 appointed by City Council and 4 appointed by the Mayor. The Committee 'Contact Person' is Daniel Krueger, City PWE; between the Mayor, her appointees, and the PWE, we have the 'Fox guarding the hen house' syndrome.

CONCLUSION:

Ballot Measure 'Proposition 1 - Houston Drainage Fee' is one big scam; conceived and unethically/unlawfully financed by private sector opportunists solely to enrich themselves; perpetrated on the citizens by self-serving conflict-of-interest politicians; promoted by an impervious-to-facts prevaricating Mayor; and currently administered by incompetents.

Houston Drainage Fee – Pie-In-The-Sky

ADDENDUM:

My further research confirms that the dubious satellite imaging technique to illustrate impervious surfaces is here to stay, and cities etc. jumping on the bandwagon to use it for revenue purposes is inevitable. In the case of Houston, my opinion is the proponents violated Texas Law on 'Specific Purpose Committees' in influencing ballot measures, and legal ethics pertaining to false advertising promoting this ballot measure, not to mention the Law of Physics pertaining to 'impervious surfaces' .

It would be impractical to attempt to penalize the Mayor, the 'Renew Houston, Inc.', and conflict-of-interest councilmen; the best route to justice appears having an appropriate and untainted Judge rule the election of Proposition 1 was invalid due to the circumstances cited, and leave the door open to properly putting it on the ballot in the next election. By that time the public will be fully aware of what they are voting for. The legal team that attempts this quest will achieve wide publicity in the media and a high-lift stepping-stone for any team member with political ambitions.

A WORD FROM OUR SPONSOR ...

This treatise is compiled by
DAN IEL W. HARBAUGH.
Houston private citizen, 85,
Graduate Engineer, WW II
Veteran, 5 tours in Vietnam as
a Military Engineer; now a Senior/Senior
citizen tired of elected politicians pandering to
opportunist charlatans peddling agendas to tap
the public's pocketbook.

56

B

www.ingramcontent.com/pod-product-compliance
Lightning Source LLC
Chambersburg PA
CBHW021923170526
45157CB00005B/2164